© Kiracofe and Kile 1984. All rights reserved.
ISBN 0-913327-01-8
ISSN 0740-4093
Library of Congress Catalog Card Number: 82-90743
Printed on 100 lb. Satin Kinfuji and 260g/m² Bon Ivory (cover) by
Nissha Printing Company, Ltd., Kyoto, Japan.
Color separations by the printer.
Book design and mechanicals completed by Kajun Graphics, San Francisco.
Typographical composition in Sabon by Gestype, San Francisco.
Editing assistance provided by Harold Nadel, Yellow Springs, Ohio.
Photographs not specifically credited were taken by Sharon Risedorph
and Lynn Kellner, San Francisco.

Kiracofe and Kile
955 Fourteenth Street
San Francisco 94114

THE QUILT DIGEST

 KIRACOFE AND KILE   SAN FRANCISCO   2

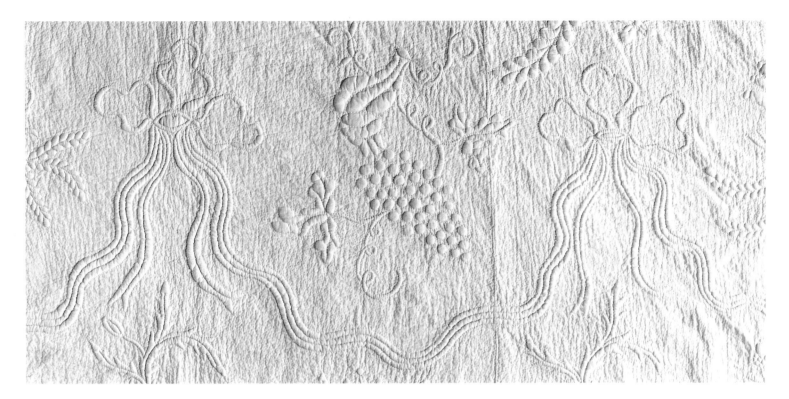

Tʜɪs has been a particularly satisfying year for us. The 1983 inaugural edition of *The Quilt Digest* sold in all fifty states and nine foreign countries. It is obvious from the mail we received that our readers are concerned, receptive quilt lovers who enjoy being challenged by new works and ideas. Our readers also seem satisfied with the start we have made. And the suggestions received from them are well considered; several have been incorporated into this second edition.

In response to popular demand, we have increased the size of *The Quilt Digest* to eighty pages. We also have added more color photography — fifty-four pages in this edition. The binding has been strengthened; it is now sewn-and-glued. And a heavier, laminated cover has been added for durability. We hope that these additions and improvements increase your enjoyment of *The Quilt Digest*.

Among the most enthusiastic and numerous comments received are those applauding the variety and mix of *The Quilt Digest*'s contents. Most noticeably, antique quilt devotees are excited and stimulated by the modern quilts reproduced in our pages, while contemporary quilt enthusiasts enjoy the historical articles on older quilts. Here is proof that quilt lovers are expanding their horizons, learning from each other.

We hope that you enjoy the variety of this edition. Once you have viewed and read it, please turn to page 78 and share your suggestions with us. For information about purchasing past, current and future editions of *The Quilt Digest*, turn to page 79 for details.

Roderick Kiracofe
Michael Kile

Contents

A Piece of

A late-nineteenth-century photograph of the Spaulding home where Ellen grew up in Ludlow, Vermont. Courtesy of Barbara Chiolino.

In the summer of 1854, inside an enormous four-story brick house at the corner of Main and Andover in Ludlow, Vermont, Ella-Elizabeth Spaulding joyously prepared for her approaching wedding and move west. Ellen, as she was called by all her friends and family, thought back to those exciting spring days several months earlier, when her first cousin Willard Reed had come from his home in Chelmsford, Massachusetts, to ask for her hand in marriage. She had known him for as long as she could remember, from his family's visits to the Spauldings. But Ellen had never known him to be so happy or enthusiastic as he was now at twenty-one, with all his plans and dreams of getting rich in the West. He had always seemed too serious, hard-working, sometimes even melancholy, and understandably so, as he had experienced frequent tragedies since a little boy. There had been so much sadness. When he was two, his mother, Leonora Spaulding Reed, had died. His father, Joseph Reed, had quickly married Maria Eaton, and then during his childhood six of his tiny half brothers and sisters had died. It was no wonder to Ellen that Willard had developed his persistent, deep-seated belief that he was "no favored child of fortune."[1]

In contrast, except for the death of her grandmother Rhoda White Spaulding in 1848, Ellen could look back on a gregarious, carefree life. Naive, even somewhat spoiled, but always fun-loving and witty, she would be an appropriate complement to Willard.

As Ellen sat cross-stitching her initials into a finely-woven cotton pillowcase, she envisioned Willard fifteen hundred miles west in Burke, Dane County, Wisconsin, building her a house and preparing for their life together. She imagined land as far as she could see — their land — and an impressive, large home in the "best of society."[2] She would be dressed in the latest fashions, and every day have ladies to tea in her own elegant home. The words printed on her calling card were symbolic of Ellen at this time in her life:

> Cheerful singing, Lively measure, voices ringing, joy and pleasure
> Lengthen out the happy day, Lengthen out the happy day.

Ellen was overjoyed. Willard had promised to return for her within several months. They would then be married and start their home together in Burke. Her new life would be full of excitement and adventure. Indeed, she had no fear now that she would be an old maid: she was going to be one of the first among her friends to marry.

But her only sister Leonora and her mother, father and grandparents, although happy for Ellen and her bright future, were sickened at the thought of her leaving and the many miles that would separate them. To ease their pain, they each made promises and plans to move to Burke soon. In the meantime, all of them wished to send something of themselves with her, a special heirloom for Ellen to keep and to remember them by. It was then that Leonora conceived of the friendship quilt. There could be no more loving, precious gift for Leonora to give her four-year-younger sister. And Leonora, her third child due in August, needed a project to keep her hands busy.

Making quilts was second nature to Leonora and Ellen, as to all the women of the Spaulding family. Their needlework skills had been passed on since their ancestor Susanna White had arrived on the Mayflower. Those early settlers had been forced through neces-

Ellen's Dress

By Linda Lipsett

sity to be self-sufficient. They had to plant flax, spin, weave and dye their own cloth, then construct their clothing. As generations passed, the Spauldings and Whites began buying some imported cloth. A receipt of February 7, 1802, from Concord, New Hampshire, records that Asa Spaulding, Leonora and Ellen's grandfather "Bo't of John White At his Variety Store, where may be had a large assortment of English and West India GOODS," indigo, copperas, and logwood dyes for their homespun, but also "3/4 yard India Cotton."

Within three more generations, spinning, weaving and dyeing cloth had become unnecessary and forgotten skills in the Spaulding family. The family could buy all the cloth they needed, so Ellen and Leonora grew up wearing dresses of fine printed cottons, silks, lawns and delaines made by their mother Arterista and grandmother Lydia Haven. The use of the needle continued to be one of their most important and necessary skills.

But now necessity joined with another aspect of needlework in America — the great pride and even vanity of fine stitches and the final creation. America's quilts reflected this: from coarsely made, home-dyed linsey-woolseys during hard times to elegant, exquisitely-stitched red and green appliques, and all-white "best" quilts during periods of comfort. Thus, the purpose of Leonora's friendship quilt was for

warmth and comfort, but not just physically: it was for the warmth and comfort of the soul.

Leonora and Ellen were not without skills of the needle. Like all girls of the time, they held the delicate tool in their tiny, clumsy fingers by four years of age, piecing together simple four-patch blocks of sprigged and flowered calicoes. They had helped thread needles while the women and older girls put their finest stitches into Grandma's latest patchwork quilt. Both girls held fond memories of the fun of a quilting. Later, what pride they had taken in being invited to sit at the frame and add their best work. The family news

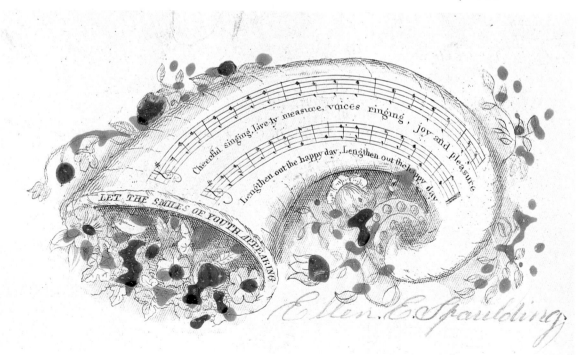

Ellen's hand-painted calling card. Courtesy of Barbara Chiolino.

and gossip of the community melted the hours away — hours that formed an integral part of their upbringing.

Soon Leonora and then Ellen were preparing for the day when they each would be "keeping house." They followed the tradition of cross-stitching their initials and numbering each of their already carefully hand-hemmed sheets and pillowcases. Leonora stitched one set in minuscule cross-stitch with fine bronze-colored silk thread. She used the lettering she had learned when making her sampler in school and recorded $\frac{L.A.S}{6}$ on each of the pillowcases. Leonora and Ellen also pieced many quilt tops for their hope chests. And before their weddings there would be "great quiltings" to transform the one-dimensional, lifeless patchwork tops magically into useful, artistic, living heirlooms.

By the spring of 1854, that period of Leonora's life was only a treasured memory. Thomas Bagley and she had been married in

Leonora's block

January 1849, when she was only seventeen. Now she had two boys and was pregnant again. Her busy life and her husband's financial difficulties had begun to show in her appearance, although she was not yet twenty-two years of age. But Leonora and her family had recently moved from their home in Reading, Vermont, into her parents' spacious brick home in Ludlow. She now had Ellen and her mother to help with the boys, and more time for her sewing and herself. She quickly became caught up in Ellen's exuberance and her own preparations for the wedding/going-away present.

Unlike the usual fashion of each participating friend making a block, signing it, then returning it to the person assembling the top, Leonora began collecting pieces of printed cottons, the cuttings of shirts and dresses of family and friends; she needed two co-ordinating fabrics for each block. The family was large, and there were also many friends and neighbors who should be included. The list grew to sixty-four: this would have to be a large quilt, with so many nine-inch blocks. Leonora had chosen the Album Patch pattern for Ellen's quilt, and began piecing the blocks with precision. She pieced her father's block from scraps her mother had saved of his clothing. Ellen's block was pieced of scraps of two of Ellen's new dresses, one of large maroon roses and rosebuds on stems, the other a soft rose, small-print calico. Every block was meaningful. Then Leonora made several blocks that were loving memorials to deceased family members: there was their grandmother Rhoda White Spaulding, and Leonora had to include Willard's mother, Leonora Spaulding Reed, who had died in 1835 at only twenty-six years of age. Hers was a special block pieced of imported, madder-dyed, hand-painted Indian cotton.

After her completion of the blocks, Leonora did not ask the sixty-four individuals to sign them, since cloth was difficult to write upon. A mistake, blob of ink or unclear signature would spoil the block, so Leonora had one person with fine penmanship (whose identity is unknown) record the name, town and state on each block. Then she set the blocks together on the diagonal with 3¼-inch sashing between them. Within several months, the top was completed and ready to be quilted. But Leonora needed a large backing. Longcloth (coarse, American-manufactured cotton resembling homespun), yardage of muslin or printed cotton normally would have been used, but that would have been expensive and not nearly as meaningful as Leonora's choice. She used her own cross-stitch-initialed linens, one darned cotton sheet and a pair of pillowcases, those that she had joyously stitched for her own hope chest years earlier. Then the backing was set in the frame, a thin cotton bat spread evenly on top of that, and finally the top. And then there was another quilting.

The months passed quickly and, without a letter of warning, Ellen's fiancé appeared at the Spaulding doorstep in Ludlow at the end of August or early in September. The Spaulding household was in a state of uproar: nothing but the quilt was ready for the trip to Wisconsin. Ellen's father had left for Burke, Wisconsin, looking over where his daughter would be living. Willard and he had unknowingly passed each other in their travels. Ellen was not packed. But Willard was impatient; his neighbors in Burke were caring for his livestock and fields, and cold weather might set in soon. The family pulled themselves together, and on September 5, 1854, nineteen-year-old Ella-Elizabeth Spaulding was married to Joseph Willard Reed. Afterwards, Ellen was presented her wedding/going-away present — Leonora's friendship quilt.

Willard believed in traveling light at the cost of practicality. He advised Ellen to take only the clothes she needed, and to have her mother send everything else. Besides a trunk of necessities, Ellen decided to take her "banbox" containing a green bonnet and another bonnet with trimmings.[3] And, of course, Ellen could not leave behind her only keepsake, the cloth album of her family and friends. The quilt was her link with all that she was leaving. The quilts and linens she had sewn for her hope chest she packed to be sent later.

Ellen's block   *Willard's block*

Album Patch, by Leonora Spaulding Bagley, Ludlow, Vermont, 1854, 91 × 96 inches, pieced American, French and English cottons with an Indian madder-dyed, hand-painted chintz. Collection of the author.

After four exhausting, bone-jarring days and nights on stages, trains, a steamboat and rigs, Ellen and Willard arrived in Burke on September 10. The next morning, she wrote to her mother and father that she and Willard "had a very pleasent time and got along well," and that her things "come safe all but the banbox and that got wet and smashed so that [her] green bonnet is spoiled and the other one wet a little."[3] But, all in all, she sounded happy with her new life and her husband's choice of land. She bragged to her parents, "I think it is as good looking place here as I have seen any where on the road and it will laugh well at the old Vermont hills and rocks in a few years when there is some good houses built for that is all that is lacking here."[3]

For several days they lived with Dolly and Abner Cady and their children in the large, two-story brick house across Portage Road from Willard's land: "We are going to stay here a few days untill we get things straitned at home and then we are going to living. the folks here look and act odd to me but they are good and very accomodading to us."[3] Then the newlyweds moved into their own home. Ellen was extremely disappointed and wrote to her sister, "we have got a little thing such as they call a house out here but it is very small, one room on the ground and one chamber, you think you are crouded to death almost, but if I had as much room as you have got, I should think I was well off."[4]

So Ellen worked in her tiny cabin, while Willard was off plowing. She washed the wooden ware from breakfast; then, in her words, "I raked up my fire soon as I got my breakfast out of the way and am sitting with the door open and am warm enough for comfort."[5] She finished her letter. Then silence. Nothingness. No one to talk to —but herself. In the distance there was the crack and deep thud of a falling tree. Ellen dwelt alone from dawn until supper. On September 16, one week after her arrival in Burke, Ellen wrote, "I have washed ironed and churned this weeke I guess you would laugh to see my great plate of butter but I did not commence setting the milk till Tuesday and churned last night [Saturday] and I got about two lbs. of butter and that is pretty well is it not for two cows <u>and one of them with a bell on her neck</u>."[4]

She also cooked meat and potatoes and baked huge loaves of wheat bread and small biscuits for tea. Her explanation of cooking in the West was, "and now I suppose you will ask when I baked, the folks do not have any sellars out this way, or at least we have not any so we live city fashion cook enough for one meel and let the next one take care of its self."[4] In addition, Ellen made cheese, fed the chickens, milked the cows, straightened her cabin, knitted stockings and sewed plain-waisted dresses for herself and shirts for Willard. It would seem she would not have time for loneliness, but one week after her arrival in Wisconsin, she wrote to her sister, "I suppose you are all guessing by this time that I am homesick but I am not for I can eat drink and sleep and folks say they can't when they are homesick but I am lonely when Willard is gone, he has been gone one other day this week a threshing for a man that he owed a days work and I expect he has got to go one day next week to work for a man on the marsh."[4] She did have one visitor that week: "There was a Norwegean woman came here this morning after Willard went away and I could not understand hardly a word she

Leonora's initials with number on the cotton sheet used as a portion of the backing.

Burke September 16th 1854,

Dear Sister Leonora

As I have a few leisure moments this after noon I will employ them in writing to you. My health is about the same as when I left home, and I hope these few lines will find you not only as well but better, and the baby (for I supose that is her name yet) and Esther too. Willard is well, he has gone out to Madison to day to get us some things for keeping house. if we had a house to keep I should not care but we have got a little thing such as they call a house out here but it is very small, one room on the ground and one chamber, you think you are crouded to death almost, but if I had as much room as you have got, I should think I was well off, but never mind we shall have more room in a year or two. You may tell Esther that Willard has gone out to get some curtains to put up around. the bed but I guess they will not be reed curtains if they are

said but at last I found out that it was a pig that she wanted so I went out with her and helped catch it and then she carried it off in her dress before real Paddy style."[4]

The lonely days seemed endless to Ellen. Weeks slowly passed without visitors, the complete opposite of her life in Vermont. Thinking back, she could not remember being alone for even one day. Her family was so large, and most of them lived within a few miles. Grandma Haven lived right around the corner, and Ellen could walk over there and help Grandma piece or quilt any time she wanted. And what Ellen would have given to visit just one of her numerous school friends. Her mother and father had warned her she would be lonely out west. Ellen had almost laughed. But then, what had she known of loneliness? Now her only conversations with other women were through letters. Letters were exchanged between Ellen and her mother and sister with two-week-old gossip and news. Occasionally, the envelopes would be thicker than usual; those were exciting ones. There were no instant photos, only fragile, expensive daguerreotypes. Besides these, the handwritten word, handmade diagrams, checks and money orders were usually all that were sent in envelopes — except for cloth. The women sent pieces of their new dresses or comforters and a drawing or pattern to illustrate the style. These pretty scraps of bright calicoes transported Ellen home for a few moments. She could envision Leonora's new dress and also include that piece in her new quilt. And back in Ludlow, Leonora and Arterista and Grandma Haven prized their pieces of Ellen's new dress or Willard's shirt. After all, these pieces were from "the far West." Never were they returned to their envelopes. The family read and reread the letters, then put them carefully back into the envelopes and saved them, but the pieces of cloth were used. These pieces of their loved ones' clothing were sewn together into precious blocks for their quilts, and were their most tangible ties to each other.

Ellen had pieced blocks and quilted since she could remember. Quilting was an integral part of her life. She was comfortable and happy at a quilting frame and now, in Wisconsin, certainly missed

Ellen's letter to Leonora, September 16, 1854. Courtesy of Barbara Chiolino.

quilting with her grandmother and the other women in the family. Through her correspondence, her mother would describe what Grandma was making, but that only made Ellen more lonely — homesick, actually, but Ellen refused to call it that.

Six weeks had painfully ended. Ellen wrote she had "not been a visiting yet nor had company but once   Mrs Cady came and spent one afternoon." But then Ellen had some relieving news for her mother: "I have been and helped her [Mrs. Cady] quilt two afternoons   she had a great quilting   there was a lot of the neighbors there and some of them spoke to me and some went home without as much as saying why do you so (as Uncle Alden said)   I expect they were affraid they should get bit."[5]

In Ellen's life in Wisconsin, that quilting at the Cadys' was her only big social event. Willard and she did not attend church services at the log school or neighbors' homes, and Ellen never mentioned actually attending a wedding or funeral, only that so-and-so had been married or died. Except on a Sunday, Willard was most likely too busy to take her. It was only a nearby quilting bee to which Ellen could go without him. Unfortunately for Ellen, within days of the quilting, the Cadys left for better virgin farmland, government land in Iowa. With Mrs. Cady went her "great quiltings."

As the plow and axe were Willard's companions in the West, the needle and pen were Ellen's. They were her means of survival, her companions in her hours of severe loneliness and depression, while her husband was away working. She tried to keep herself busy with needlework after completing her other household duties. In spite of solitude, she found contentment in her accomplishments: "I am footing a pair of stockings for myself now,. . .and have made Willard a pair of pants and he fetched home cloth for another pair last night, so you see I am jack at all traids."[6] And besides all of her other sewing, she was also piecing quilts. She wrote on March 19, 1856, "I am pieceing me a comfortable, called Boneparts retreat."[7]

Ellen grew more and more intensely homesick and longed to be a part of her family's get-togethers, especially the quiltings. Her mother was beginning a comfortable and sent Ellen a piece. In another letter Ellen wrote, "I think your dress and aprons very

pretty, and Grandmas quilt." Ellen deeply meant it when she added, "I wish I could come and help her quilt it."[8]

There was no hope of a quilting invitation in the West for Ellen now. Willard had grown dissatisfied and moved her to virgin land with more wood and water, about eighty-five miles northwest in Glendale Township, Juneau County, Wisconsin. Once again her husband was engulfed in clearing, grubbing, breaking and fencing, leaving Ellen from dawn until dusk to occupy herself. The nearest town was Mauston, sixteen miles away, but the supplies there were limited. Willard had to go nearly a hundred miles back to Madison for a good selection of calico and other printed cottons for Ellen's new dresses and quilts. And Ellen always wrote home proudly about a new dress and sent a piece for her mother and grandmother. Each piece of cloth now became precious to Ellen. She had to wait months for Willard to surprise her with more. Besides, even the purchase of cloth was a sacrifice to them now that there were such "hard times"[9] throughout the western country. Ellen was forced to make her tiny scraps last. She began piecing blocks for another quilt.

But the depression of 1857 had much more serious results than a shortage of cloth for Ellen and Willard. There was a severe shortage of food and other material necessities. "Money is very scarce out here, and all kinds of grain is down low and every thing we have to buy is very high and we can not get trusted to the stores any, (and I am glad of that), so we can live without. . . .we have not had any meat lately, nor a speck of butter for weeks and weeks, there is none

A late-nineteenth-century photograph of Ludlow, Vermont. Courtesy of Barbara Chiolino.

in the country to be bought, so there it is again, and we cant get a cow till we get some money so we live on potatoe and salt with a little milk on it, and bread without butter, and have lived weeks this summer without a speck of sugar in the house, and have three or four ladies some out from Mauston, and nothing for tea but biscuit and a little butter I had some then and tea, but that is nothing it is out wist in the land that flows with milk and honey."[9]

No longer was Ellen immature or naive. The three years in the West had forced her to grow up quickly and to perceive life in a serious vein. And Ellen was also brave. For several years she had continued to go about as normally as she could with a "hard cough." But with her poor diet and loneliness resulting in deep depression, her condition had continually grown worse, and she wrote, "My health has been very poor ever since I came out here [Glendale] last fall, and I do not think it is much better nor looks very incourageing for me. I have a very hard cough all of the time, and have had hard colds one after the other all summer and fall. I am takeing Wisters Balsom of wild Cherry and think it helps me some, and would a great deel more if I had half a chance for my life, but you think it is hard times there where you have enough of every thing, but I guess if you was out here as we, and thousands of others have been, you would not call that hard, but we have been obliged to live so because we could not get our money for things that we sold nor where it was due us."[9]

Ellen's gravestone, Ludlow, Vermont.

In spite of her poor, fragile condition, Ellen had not forgotten to include another swatch of cotton in a letter two weeks earlier: "that piece I sent you in his [Willard's] letter was a piece of my new dress." And she continued, "I have got my knitting and sewing most done, I have done my work with what Willard helps me, all but my washing. I have not washed a thing but twice since early last spring, and you need not think it is the seven nor nine month consumption that ails me either, if you do you are mistaken."[9]

In April 1858, after nearly four years of Ellen's invitations and pleading, her parents finally arrived at their children's newly completed two-story "house made of Popple logs"[9] in Glendale Township, Wisconsin. Stedman and Arterista, unsuspecting of the seriousness of Ellen's illness, were shocked by their daughter's emaciated body, her critical state.

For three months they nursed her. Her compassionate father "mooved her from one bed to the other"[10] several times in the day, trying to make her more comfortable. Stedman wrote that "Ellen had sustained the idea that her disorder was not the consumption and that she should get better by and by and be able to return to Vermont with us next fall or winter which She ever expressed considerable anxiety for doing. and when her flesh and strength was so gone that she could not set in her chair nor bear her weight on her feet she thought still that she would start to go home if we would go with her, but the Doctor said her lungs were so much deceyed that the moment we went to mooving her they would break down and she would certainly die."[10]

Despite her family's loving care and companionship, Ellen's death was inevitable, and "she breathed out her last gust, Monday Eight-Oclock in the after noon,"[10] July 12, 1858, one month before her twenty-third birthday.

When Ellen Reed died, she did not have many possessions, and fewer still of value from her dour western existence. There were only some personal articles and her quilts. Upon her deathbed, she asked her parents to give those quilts to members of the family. Eight months after her death, Willard's father thanked Stedman and Arterista Spaulding: "Ellens quilts came safe and were very gladly receivd by us and also Charles and Emily rec'd thiers with

LINDA LIPSETT

great pleasure." Then Maria Reed added, "we received Ellens kind presant and feel very much pleased with them and feell very greatful to you for your trouble and hope I can repay you someetime."[11]

And Ellen's wedding gift from her sister, her cherished friendship quilt, was returned to her sister.

There was one more request Ellen made of her parents. When she had accepted her fast-approaching death, Ellen requested they "take her remains back to Ludlow."[10] So on April 18, 1859, nine months after her death, Ellen's body was finally laid to rest in the quiet, secluded cemetery on the hill, only one long block from her family's home in Ludlow, Vermont.

While still in Glendale, Wisconsin, Ellen's father had written to Leonora, "I hope they [his grandchildren] will all of them remember her so that she will not be forgotten by them."[12] One hundred and twenty-six years have passed since Stedman's letter to Leonora. The brick home at the corner of Main and Andover is gone; a post office stands in its place. Willard's years of toil in constructing log houses, barns, and rail fences have slowly been erased from the Wisconsin landscape. Only the letters and Ellen's friendship quilt survive so we can relive Ellen's story and see a piece of Ellen's dress.

The story you have just read is not fiction. Every detail was uncovered by the author in forgotten letters, government records, genealogy charts and newspapers of the day. Ellen Spaulding Reed's story is rare and unusual only because it has been told; there are millions of such stories, vivid recollections of our shared American past, left to be discovered by caring, dedicated people. In her article in last year's The Quilt Digest, *Julie Silber stated, "I have long believed that quilts, the work of hands, are among our richest tools in uncovering the lives and experiences of everyday women in an earlier America." The telling of Ellen's story started with her quilt and a modern-day woman who wanted to know more about it. Thanks to Linda Lipsett, another piece of American history has been recovered. Ideally, other quilt enthusiasts will use this article as inspiration for similar undertakings.* —Michael Kile

REFERENCE LIST

1. J.W. Reed to Stedman and Arterista Spaulding, from Plymouth, Wisconsin to Ludlow, Vermont, August 17, 1862.

2. Description of Dane County, in the *Wisconsin Gazetteer,* Madison, Wisconsin, 1853.

3. Ellen E. Reed to Stedman and Arterista Spaulding, from Burke, Wisconsin, September 11, 1854.

4. To Leonora Bagley, September 16, 1854.

5. To Arterista Spaulding, October 27, 1854.

6. To Stedman and Arterista Spaulding, September 25, 1855.

7. To Stedman and Arterista Spaulding (continuation of letter begun by J.W. Reed), March 17-19, 1856.

8. To Stedman and Arterista Spaulding, from Glendale Township, Wisconsin, May 13, 1857.

9. To Stedman and Arterista Spaulding, October 25, 1857.

10. Stedman Spaulding to Thomas and Leonora Bagley, from Glendale Township, Wisconsin to Reading, Vermont, July 15, 1858.

11. Joseph and Maria Reed to Stedman and Arterista Spaulding, from Chelmsford, Massachusetts to Ludlow, Vermont, March 21, 1860.

12. Stedman Spaulding to Thomas and Leonora Bagley, from Glendale Township, Wisconsin to Reading, Vermont, August 18, 1858.

LINDA LIPSETT, a violist who lives in Los Angeles, is a studio musician for movies, television and recordings. She is also a member of the Los Angeles Chamber Orchestra, a quilt historian and quilt collector. Her collection consists of quilts which, like the one chronicled here, she has researched. She has traveled the country, covering thousands of miles, tracing the origins of her quilts. She is currently at work on a book-length version of this article.

LOOKING TOWARD THE FUTURE

THE COLLECTOR

By Michael Kile

THE current revival of interest in antique quilts owes its existence to a wide variety of people and circumstances. Strangely, one of the least acknowledged and understood phenomena is the contribution of private collectors. Their eager willingness to purchase and accumulate America's antique quilts has been the foundation upon which the panoply of exhibitions and books has been mounted. Without the constantly growing interest by individuals willing to pay ever-increasing sums of money for an ever-dwindling supply of heirloom quilts, this revival might have slowed or ceased several years ago.

There is no doubt that museums, dealers, the press and the general public have played their instrumental roles in this revival, but none seems as essential as that of the individual collector. Museums have served as caretakers of our nation's quilts for decades but, as any weary textile curator will confirm, few have allocated sufficient resources to protect their collections, let alone purchase the quilts that have appeared on the market in the past ten years. In fact, dealers have unearthed a staggering number of antique quilts, many of which have headlined exhibitions, initiating interest in the press and general public. But it has been the private collectors who have fed this interest with their willingness to purchase heirloom after heirloom. How many private collectors there are is anyone's guess, but they must number in the tens of thousands. After all, besides the thousands of American collectors, others have come here, bought quilts, and returned home to Europe and Asia with their new-found treasures. Collecting America's quilts is truly an international obsession.

Private collectors are as varied as their collections. Most simply buy, in whatever numbers their checkbooks will allow, quilts that appeal to them. Still others focus on one region's heirlooms or a particular style or type. And a few, luckily, have the foresight, ambition and income to attempt the most difficult task: forming a comprehensive collection that adequately surveys American quiltmaking of the past, from the earliest quilts to those completed during the Depression, a stretch of one hundred and fifty years.

Edwin Binney, 3rd and his daughter, Gail Binney-Winslow, are such collectors. As a father-daughter collecting team, they may be unique in the quilt world, but equally rare are their credentials: Ed is an accomplished collector in several fields, having written the catalogues for numerous museum exhibitions, while Gail is a quiltmaker and teacher of the craft. Thus, they bring to their collecting task talents and experiences of which few collectors can boast.

Ed is what many who know him describe correctly as a "professional collector." In fact, his collecting started at an early age while he traveled extensively with his mother. He began hoarding hotel soaps and, to this day, has their wrappers displayed in his study. While in the service during World War II, he was an interpreter for Japanese prisoners of war and started collecting military dog tags. Today his collections include an important assemblage of Turkish and Indian miniature paintings and the largest known

Original design, c. 1880-1900, found in Ohio, 68½ × 87½ inches, appliqued cottons.

holding of nineteenth-century ballet prints. He has lectured on these collections around the world. He is a trustee of the San Diego Museum of Art, where the Binney quilt collection is stored, and a former trustee of the Portland (Oregon) Art Museum.

Gail studied painting and printmaking before she discovered quiltmaking. In the mid-1970's she owned and operated The Nine Patch, a quilt shop in San Diego, and taught quiltmaking to students in the area. Three years ago she returned home to Cape Cod, married and now lives in a two-hundred-year-old house on land that was granted to her husband's family before the Revolutionary War. She has created a studio in part of the house and has a thriving business designing and making quilts and one-of-a-kind clothing.

Ed and Gail started collecting quilts on a trip to Portland in 1970. Gail, then a young adult, remembers the trip vividly: "We went to visit the Oregon State Historical Society. There was a quilt there that was made by Dad's great-great-grandmother, an Oregon pioneer. I had a very strong reaction to it. I immediately started searching out other quilts. Soon thereafter, I opened The Nine Patch and

Princess Feather, c. 1875-1900, Pennsylvania, 88½ × 91½ inches, appliqued and pieced cottons.

18

began dealing in quilts. Dad became more and more interested in what I was doing. He's an inveterate collector and I don't think he could stand seeing all these quilts and not be involved. We started buying quilts for each other on holidays and one another's birthdays. The collection grew from there."

According to Ed, Gail's shop gave them the opportunity to view and assess many quilts. It was an educating experience for him. "Initially," Gail adds, "Dad knew very little about quilts. I would show him a quilt and say, 'Now, this is a very good example.' If he liked it, he would reply, 'Then maybe we should have that one.' Dad is an intellectual collector and I'm an instinctive one. I collect to create an environment in which I am comfortable. He collects as an intellectual exercise. Dad spends a great deal of time researching sources and reading whatever is available on the subject. He's an investigator. I, on the other hand, love to study fabrics, stitches and techniques. Dad looks for bright colors and I like the earthy ones. He looks at graphics and dynamics and I'm down with my nose in the quilt, counting stitches. If you've never sewed,

Tumbling Blocks variation, c. 1875-1900, origin unknown, 75½ × 90½ inches, pieced silks and velvets.

Album, c. 1854, from the George Washington MacKay Young family, Baltimore, Maryland, 105½ × 106 inches, appliqued cottons. Techniques include trapunto, padding and embroidery. As in many such quilts, this one possesses a block composed of Odd Fellows symbols. "F.L.T," for example, stands for the order's credo: Friendship, Love and Truth. For a more detailed description of this quilt and its history, consult *Baltimore Album Quilts* by Dena S. Katzenberg, published by The Baltimore Museum of Art, page 118.

you can't help but look at graphics. If you sew, you first look at stitches."

This difference of tastes and attitudes could wreck any co-operative venture, particularly something as subjective as collecting, but in their case it seems to have proven a positive influence. "Gail is a wonderfully creative quiltmaker. I respect my daughter's expertise. She knows the craft required to design and construct a fine quilt. Because of her, I am a far better appreciator of craft than I was at the beginning. But I look at quilts as an aesthetic experience. My accent is always on color and design, in that order. Then, later, I look at craft. I like bright colors on a white background. Gail is apt to go for brown calico prints. I tend toward the elegant, Gail favors the folksy. We're a mixed bag."

"There are many collections that have focused successfully on one particular kind of quilt. That's impossible for us to do. We're both too eclectic and our tastes are far too wide-ranging," Gail admits. "Besides, focusing the collection on a particular type or style would ruin our fun. The most important thing about the collection is that it is a shared joy and commitment for Dad and me. We approach it differently, but we share in it. We tend to balance each other because we are drawn to quilts for different rea-

sons." Ed agrees: "We started collecting because Gail had found her vocation in quiltmaking and I was interested in doing something with my adult daughter."

EVERY collector has at least a subconscious goal in mind for a collection. With the Binneys, it is out in the forefront. "Our goal has changed a number of times," says Gail. "When we started we didn't have any idea we were looking to collect a broad range of American quiltmaking. At least, I didn't. I was collecting quilts for which I had an emotional response. My personal goal now is to gather a collection that will be meaningful, something we can leave behind as a representative history of American quiltmaking. And, let's face it, that's a tough assignment." Ed, on the other hand, remembers when there were only six quilts and he was already looking for examples to fill in the gaps. "I'm always looking for a unity of the whole. I have recently begun to see the collection as one that represents a broad cross-section of American quiltmaking. The collection has grown to a point where such a thought is at least possible. After all, we just catalogued our one-hundred-and-first quilt.

"I have always been willing to buy pieces, for any of my collections, that

haven't particularly appealed to me, but that were needed. A collector must do this. Gail's approach is far more personal. She finds it difficult to acquire a quilt just because we should have it to represent a particular period or style. She favors works she loves. But we both recognize that the collection is an important one. There are enough great works in this collection that it has potential, but it also has depth. Any good collection must be more important than the sum of its individual parts."

Their collection is now at a point of reassessment. They are selling works from it, replacing lesser with finer examples and building strengths in some areas while winnowing out too large a preponderance in others. Ed seems particularly to enjoy this process. "If we get to a point where everything is perfect and our goal is reached, however, my interest will wane," he admits. Gail, on the other hand, many times finds this collector's duty difficult to accomplish: "Quilts are sometimes special to me for the circumstances in which we bought them, or because of whom we bought them from. It saddens me when I realize that we have outgrown some quilts, that our requirements have become stricter."

They both seem comfortable with their assessments of the collection. Both agree on which quilts are the most important. "Not a hard task, after all," Gail admits. And they both readily agree on which is their favorite group in the collection. "My real loves are the cobalt-blue-and-whites. It seems that any reasonably prolific quiltmaker alive between 1840 and 1900 made at least one such quilt. Almost always they are geometrics, rarely are they complicated patterns and most are exceptionally well-quilted. I've never met anyone who dislikes cobalt-blue-and-white quilts. Even people who don't know quilts react favorably towards them. They are so unconfusing, so aesthetically pleasing. They are soothing to the soul." Ed agrees, adding, "They are our meeting ground. We both love them. They are so elegant and yet they possess utter simplicity."

B EGINNING collectors often search for an explanation of their mad, growing obsession. Ed Binney, who has been a collector for decades, doesn't hesitate when asked for a definition of a collector: "A nut!" he replies. "Someone who feels his or her own desire for self-expression has an educative value for others over and

Double Inside Border, c. 1920-1940, Ohio Amish, 80 × 63½ inches, pieced cotton sateens.

above the specific enjoyment received as a collector. All collectors should think they are the embodiment of this definition, but you see that's the problem: individual collections are as varied as their creators. I go my way collecting, knowing only how *I* feel about things. Sometimes, many times, Gail and I feel differently about a quilt, but both of us agree on possessing it. This is a very personal exercise."

"This whole thing is very personal to me," Gail adds. "I collect because I so respect the works and the women who created them. Here were all these women, virtually none of them with formal educations, and they stitched one of America's greatest creative legacies. As a quiltmaker, I look to old quilts for inspiration. A collector should gain intellectual stimulation from the task of collecting. That's very important. These old quilts inspire me to do something different in my own work. When following traditional patterns, I have an obligation to add my own aesthetic interpretations, which will, in the future, reflect our time. Sadly, I think most modern-day quiltmakers try only to reproduce what they see in old quilts. I *know* I can't do better, so I don't try. If you've seen the best of antique quilts, you know there's no sense to try and reproduce them.

"You can't help but educate yourself as you go along. We've started sharing the collection with others in exhibitions and lectures. I've learned how little the public knows about the history and evolution of quiltmaking. I feel as though I am actively connecting the past with the present. That's an important duty for any collector."

Ed, who has created and cultivated numerous collections, says he is particularly enthusiastic about quilts. "I now

---

Linsey-woolsey, by Eunice Farrer Chamberlain, near Plattsburgh, New York, c. 1800, 100 × 102 inches, pieced and glazed.

stand in awe of the incredible aesthetic intuition of nineteenth-century American women. Most had no professional training or knowledge, but several produced masterpieces. At the beginning, I did not recognize a masterpiece quilt as I could a masterpiece painting. I did not know they existed; now I do."

Gail adds a somber thought, however. "I can't help but wonder," she says, "what will happen after us. I hope all collectors are thinking about this, and making adequate preparations. There are so few museums with adequate storage facilities, and so few homes that have proper storage cabinets. What a shame: to spend a lifetime collecting, not knowing your collection is in jeopardy, and to have no place to leave it safely after you are gone. We must educate the public, and specifically enthusiasts, if we are to safeguard our quilts. I see things beginning to happen. For example, right here in our area, the New England Quilt Guild has started making long-range plans for a regional center where quilts can be shown, cared for and studied. They are also acquiring works by accomplished contemporary quiltmakers, conserving them from the start so someone won't

Carpenter's Square, c. 1880-1900, eastern United States, 79 × 79 inches, pieced cottons.

have to rescue them from garage floors a hundred years from now. But the process is slow and it is so easy to avoid this issue. What we really need is a national museum, or a series of museum centers across the country, but that is a long way off. Women have expressed their creativity in quilts generation after generation. They made them with care, skill and love, taking months or years on a single quilt. That's an incredible statement about women, their patience and their aesthetic. We can't let their creations go unprotected."

I T is obvious to anyone in the antique quilt field that our private collectors are integral to the preservation and enjoyment of our quilt heritage. In sheer numbers alone, they possess the vast majority of antique quilts sold to date. Not much has been said on this subject; it is a vital question without simple answers. Luckily, there are collectors like the Binneys who are not only acquiring quilts, but thinking about the future when they themselves are gone but the quilts, we all hope, remain.

Variable Star with central medallion motif, c. 1840-1860, eastern United States, 75½ × 91 inches, pieced and appliqued cottons. Some of the applique is padded.

VICTORIAN STYLE, with its excessive design and decoration, developed during a period in which America was changing from an insular, slumbering giant into a world power with great influence. With this emergence came the realization that worlds exist beyond our shores, exciting worlds of opulent and bizarre artifacts. The American Victorians were enthralled by these new lands and objects, and their lifestyle proclaimed this enchantment.

The photographs which follow were taken near the turn of the century in Chicago's well-to-do Gold Coast district. Today a large printing factory occupies most of this area. The house belonged to the Moulton family and stood at 2119 Calumet Avenue. The Moultons were obviously so proud of their environment that they hired a professional photographer to chronicle its details.

And what details they were. The house is crammed with Victorian excess: a skull wearing military headgear, fans of

Victorian Style

VINTAGE PHOTOGRAPHS OF AN AMERICAN HOME

every type and description, a whisk broom mounted on steer horns and a crazy quilt on every bed. Items such as these were

the result of do-it-yourself decorating projects at a time when home decoration was a serious avocation for every Victorian

woman. The Victorian housewife, regardless of her economic conditions, believed that the polish of tasteful surroundings would rub off on family members. Books on decorating encouraged women — at times sternly goaded them — to turn lackluster rooms into visions of Victorian delight. "We hold that any woman of ordinary strength, and enjoying an average of usual health, may by management of details, and judicious expenditure of time, make for herself and those she loves a home, beautiful in embellishment, and furnished with comparative luxury."[1]

Embellishment was clearly the watchword to a successful decorating scheme, and women collected travel souvenirs and trinkets to add to growing collections of whatever caught their fancy. A writer in *Harper's Bazar* mentions one woman whose hunger for teapots could not be satisfied until she had collected three hundred to brighten her drawing room.[2] If money was scarce, housewives could count on a burgeoning number of women's magazines to be full of thrifty, if not tasty, recipes ("Jelly from Old Boots"[3]), armchair-travel articles on exotic lands and cultures ("Physical Strength of Savages"[4]), as well as patterns and directions for turning such raw materials as shells, seaweed, eggshells, feathers, human hair, fabric scraps, dried weeds and broken umbrellas into tastefully functional chair tidies, pen wipers, wall plaques, negligee bags, wall-pockets ("probably no other article of modern invention and ingenuity has afforded greater satisfaction than wall-pockets"[5]) and washstand mats.

The magazines also created a passion for what became the finishing touch to many rooms: the crazy quilt. Suddenly the fashionable young ladies who would never have thought of piecing a quilt were coveting one another's scraps. As *The Delineator* magazine reported in 1883, "Ten years ago the patchwork quilt was relegated to the busy bees of the house-

Front of 2119 Calumet Ave. Chicago, Ill.

hold; today the butterflies are so eager for it they absolutely stop playing and go to work."[6]

You enter the American Victorian age — via the Moulton home — by turning the page. Take your time: there is much to see. — PENNY MCMORRIS

REFERENCE LIST

1. Mrs. C.S. Jones and Henry Williams, *Beautiful Homes: How to Make Them* (New York: Henry S. Allen, 1885), p. 7.

2. *Harper's Bazar,* 26 Aug. 1882, p. 530.

3. "Jelly from Old Boots," *Godey's Lady's Book,* Oct. 1877, p. 351.

4. "Physical Strength of Savages," *Godey's Lady's Book,* Aug. 1877, p. 173.

5. Jones and Williams, p. 139.

6. *The Delineator,* Aug. 1883, p. 116.

PENNY MCMORRIS created, produced and hosted two PBS television series, *Quilting* and *Quilting II.* Her full-length book, *Crazy Quilts,* appeared in April 1984. A resident of Bowling Green, Ohio, she has lectured throughout the United States on a wide variety of quilt subjects. She also serves as art curator for Owens-Corning Fiberglas of Toledo, Ohio.

THE Moulton home photographs are from the quilt memorabilia collection of *The Quilt Digest.* The stamp "Spencer, Photographer, 7520 Ellis Ave., Chicago," as well as a hand-written caption, appears on the back of each photograph; these have been reproduced exactly.

Reception room & hall

Drawing room -

29

Mr & Mrs Moulton room

30

Grandmas room.

Mein Moulton zim -

32

Master Moulton's room

SHOWCASE

COMPILED BY RODERICK KIRACOFE

Star of Bethlehem, by
Glendora Hutson,
Berkeley, California,
1980, 53 × 53 inches,
hand-appliqued and
machine-pieced printed
cottons. Hand-quilted by
Gayle Larson, Vallejo,
California. Initialed and
dated in embroidery.
Collection of Glendora
Hutson.

Inscription, by Cornelia Catharine Vosburgh, Red Hook, New York, 1874-1876, 102 × 80 inches, pieced cottons. Dated "1876" in the quilting. Beginning at the outer bottom left corner of the quilt, the inscription reads: "Cornelia Catharine Vosburgh Red Hook Dec 25 1874 May the blessing of God await thee & FROM EVERY QUARTER FLOWING JOYFUL CROWDS ASSEMBLE ROUND AND SPAKE WITH EXALTED ZEAL." This message is proof of the quiltmaker's determination to include the entire alphabet in her work. Several Inscription quilts have survived, but few possess all twenty-six letters. For a more detailed discussion of this quilt, consult Winifred Reddall's article in *Uncoverings 1980,* published by American Quilt Study Group, Mill Valley, California. Private collection.

Rising Sun variation, c. 1860-1870, origin unknown, 89 × 88 inches, pieced and appliqued cottons. Minnesota Historical Society Museum Collections, St. Paul.

Orange Construction,
by David Hornung,
Saratoga Springs, New
York, 1982, 55 × 68
inches, hand-appliqued,
pieced and quilted by
machine in cottons and
polished cottons. Collec-
tion of Michael James.

Railroad Crossing, by
Elizabeth A. Yoder,
Mount Hope, Holmes
County (Ohio) Amish,
c. 1880-1900, 76 × 40
inches, pieced cottons.
Collection of Darwin
Bearley, Akron, Ohio.

38

JOHN COLES

Mirrored Steps, by Pauline Burbidge, Nottingham, England, 1983, 79 × 83 inches, pieced and quilted by machine in cottons, some of which are hand-dyed. This quilt was designed from cardboard models of steps made by the quiltmaker, placed in front of two mirrors. Collection of the quilt-maker.

39

Twilight Zones, © July 1983 Esther Parkhurst, Los Angeles, 80 × 51 inches, cottons strip-pieced by machine, quilted by hand. Collection of the quilt-maker.

Black Egg Man, by
Jean Hewes, Los Gatos,
California, 1981,
42 × 62 inches, machine-
appliqued cottons, rayons
and polyester silks.
Quilted by hand and
machine. Machine-
stitched signature and
date. Collection of
the quiltmaker.

Impressions de France,
by Françoise Barnes,
Athens, Ohio, 1983,
72 × 63 inches, machine-
pieced and hand-quilted
cottons and cotton
blends. Collection of the
quiltmaker.

Log Cabin — Barn Raising variation, c. 1875-1900, Oley Valley, Berks County, Pennsylvania, 73 × 80 inches, cottons. Collection of Don Leiby, Hamburg, Pennsylvania.

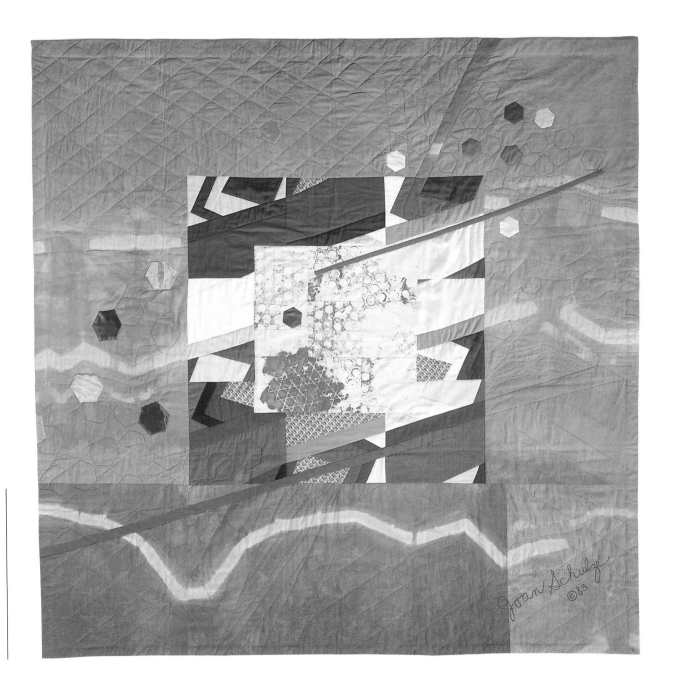

Lunch at the Flamingo Palace, © 1983 Joan Schulze, Sunnyvale, California, 72 × 71 inches, appliquéd and pieced cottons, silks and satins, hand-dyed and painted. Quilted by hand and machine. Signed and dated in embroidery. Collection of the quilt-maker.

Seek-No-Further, by Bernice Enyeart, Huntington, Indiana, 1980, 84 × 83 inches, appliqued and pieced cottons. Signed, dated and numbered in embroidery. This is the quiltmaker's rendition of a quilt of the same pattern name found in *Old Patchwork Quilts* by Ruth E. Finley. Collection of the quiltmaker.

45

Deer Dancers at San Ildefons Pueblo, © 1983 Terrie Hancock Mangat, Cincinnati, Ohio, 102 × 101 inches, machine-pieced and hand-appliqued cottons and cotton blends, with embroidery floss, old lace, porcupine quills, glass beads, metal balls, floss tassels, sequins and an old silk tie. Techniques include reverse applique and embroidery. Hand-quilted by Sue Rule, Carlisle, Kentucky. Titled, signed and dated in embroidery. This quilt was inspired by a visit to the New Mexican pueblo where Mangat witnessed the ritual of the Deer Dance. Collection of Terrie Hancock Mangat.

Single Irish Chain, by
Dora Bales Planck, Great
Bend, Kansas, c. 1920,
80 × 80 inches, pieced
cottons. Collection of
Mrs. Ruth B. Clark,
daughter of the quilt-
maker.

Liquorice Allsorts, by Pauline Burbidge, Nottingham, England, 1983, 88 × 95 inches, pieced and quilted by machine in cottons, most of which are hand-dyed. This quilt was designed from cardboard models made by the quiltmaker, placed in front of two mirrors. The title refers to a type of English candy. Collection of the quiltmaker.

Missouri River Scene,
© 1980 Chris Wolf
Edmonds, Lawrence,
Kansas, 46 × 42 inches,
appliqued and pieced
cottons and cotton blends.
The border frame is
composed of a traditional
pattern, Missouri Wonder.
Private collection.

#26, by Pam Studstill, Pipe Creek, Texas, 1983, 39 × 40 inches, whole-cloth center surrounded by four-patch border. Machine-pieced and hand-quilted cottons which are dyed and painted by hand. Signed and numbered in embroidery. Collection of the quiltmaker.

Floral Urns, 1856, found in Iowa, 81 × 82 inches, appliqued cottons. Techniques include stuffed work, reverse applique, piping, embroidery and stipple quilting. Initialed "L.C." and dated in the center of the quilt. Collection of Barbara S. Janos and Barbara Ross. (See cover for a detail of this quilt.)

#28, by Pam Studstill, Pipe Creek, Texas, 1983, 48 × 48 inches, machine-pieced and hand-quilted cottons which are commercially dyed and painted by hand. Signed and numbered in embroidery. Collection of the quiltmaker.

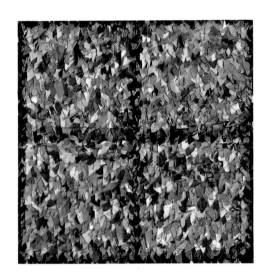

Victorian silk work,
c. 1880-1900, found in
Maryland, 60 × 61
inches, silks, velvets and
satins. Individually-cut
pieces are sewn in layers
to a ground cloth, backed
with a printed cotton.
Collection of Yvonne
Porcella.

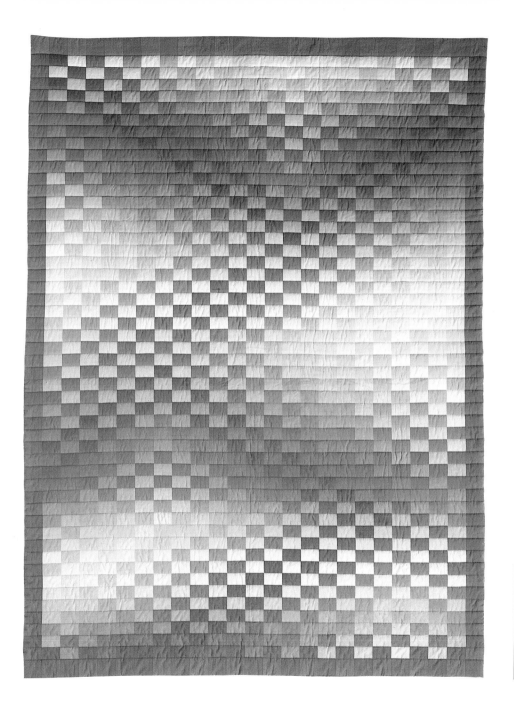

Diagonal Study II,
© 1983 Jan Myers,
Minneapolis, 56 × 77
inches, pieced and quilted
by machine in cotton
muslins, hand-dyed with
procion dyes. Collection
of the quiltmaker.

Dairy Queen Salt and Pepper Shakers, by Therese May, Los Gatos, California, 1981, 51 × 38 inches, cottons, cotton sateens and velvets machine-appliqued to a canvas, backed with cotton sateen. Tacked by hand with buttons. A photograph taken by the quiltmaker is the inspiration for this work. Collection of the quiltmaker.

Crazy, by Rozina Ecker Adams, Cooperstown, North Dakota, 1899-1902, 67 × 83 inches, pieced and appliqued cottons. Techniques include reverse applique and embroidery. There are over 11,600 pieces of fabric in this quilt. Collection of Donald Kirkeby. Courtesy of The Country Arts Collective, Fargo, North Dakota.

The Collector's Guide for the Care of Quilts in the Home

OBSERVERS of twentieth-century cultural patterns will, no doubt, comment on the custom of individuals to exhibit connoisseurship through the assemblage of large collections of objects. It has not been unusual for collectors of American folk art, for example, to have gathered hundreds of artifacts around them in the informality of their homes. The domestic landscape, therefore, becomes the repository for new collections which might have previously been collected by and housed in institutions.

This proliferation of extensive collections has obliged collectors to preserve these artifacts, a difficult task in a setting which may be highly conducive to their deterioration. Homes create conservation problems not generally present in museum collections. Private premises provide a natural setting in which objects are displayed in the manner of their collectors' tastes and attitudes. The free or formal arrangement of artifacts in a living atmosphere places them in the path of constant deterioration. Living with these objects, in one sense, means using them up.

By Patsy Orlofsky

In a domestic setting, objects are permanently on display and are permanently subjected to light, climatic changes, dirt and dust, infestation and occasional handling. If textiles are already weak with age, the detrimental effect of these factors becomes an important process to arrest. The experience of professional conservators in museum settings has provided us with a body of techniques for dealing with these adverse conditions, some of which can be adapted to the needs of the private collector. I have developed this brief guide in hope that it will encourage many private collectors to think about serious care and preservation of their quilts.

Before you can make any specific decisions about exhibiting or storing individual quilts, you should create a healthy environment. To create such an environment, you must consider climate control, light, pest control and cleaning; such concerns as airborne particulate matter, humidity changes and ultraviolet light rays are all very real problems, not abstractions created by conservators.

Climate Control

Climate control encompasses the regulation of temperature and humidity, and air ventilation and filtration. Unfortunately, temperature and humidity can be quite difficult to control in a domestic setting. In a museum, a 45% to 55% relative humidity and a temperature of 55° to 65° Fahrenheit are considered optimal, with the less variation the better. Temperature and humidity work together. A rapidly changing temperature, even without a loss or gain in actual humidity, causes a change in relative humidity, that is, the amount of moisture held in the air. A rapid decrease in temperature, for example, causes the air to drop its moisture, resulting in condensation on cooler surfaces. This sort of change can cause water stains on a quilt with glass or metal in its framing. Humidity is a complicated problem since, ideally, the air should be neither too dry nor too damp, and conditions should not vary more than 5% around a stable level (preferably 50% relative humidity).

Unstable humidity is a very serious problem in many areas of the United States. The Southeast, both coasts and Hawaii suffer from unusually high humidity, constant moisture, heavy salt concentrations from oceanic waters and rapid fluctuations from wetness to dryness, and back again. Dyes actually fade more rapidly in these conditions, and dampness encourages mildew and other molds, bacteria and water staining. Good air circulation and a median relative humidity (50%) level are needed to maintain a safe, stable environment. Probably the very best and simplest protective measure against fungi is the continuous movement of air by fans. In addition, for rooms without any kind of humidity control, some good and little harm can come from judicious opening of windows in good weather and closing of them during unfavorable conditions.[1] The purchase of a hygrometer which can be placed next to a quilt or in a storage cabinet is sensible. Such a device will help you monitor the humidity of any area in which your quilts are kept.

If a textile has gotten wet through excessive humidity build-up, leakage or rain coming in through a window, relatively fast drying from the wet state may be important to inhibit mold growth.[2] Drying within an hour or two is a safe time frame for textiles. Fans can be employed, or drying can be done outdoors on a clean, dry surface out of direct sunlight. A damp wall on which a quilt is hung may encourage mold growth on the back of the quilt. In this case, the quilt should be moved and the area should be ventilated. If the damp conditions persist, a false inner wall or partition should be erected. Often an electrical heater will cure a dampness problem.[3] Make certain, however, that the heater is kept a safe distance from the quilt. And, finally, a dehumidifier can dramatically alter a damp environment.

Overly dry conditions can cause embrittlement or cracking of fibers. Since natural fibers expand to hold moisture and then contract when dried, rapid or continuous changes place strain on the fibers themselves. Shrinking, swelling and movement of fibers create a special strain when different fiber types exist in the same textile.[4] Excessive radiant and conducted heat is also damaging; objects too near radiators or in damp surroundings can become brittle or badly stained. A humidifier can help to raise the humidity level. In some cases, a strategically placed bowl of water can help.

While most of us are unable to afford ideal climatic controls, a portable humidifier, hygrometer, dehumidifier, air conditioner, heater and fan are useful instruments we can employ to alter a hazardous environment.

Air filtration is a concern for collectors in urban areas. Filtration means cleaning the air of physical and chemical soils. Physical soil is particulate matter, dust, food, grease from hands and hair, soot, lint, pollen and bugs. Chemical soil is gaseous matter (such as gases from pollution) which can be very dangerous but difficult to control without expensive equipment. To control physical soil is somewhat easier. It really means a constant program of keeping things clean: vacuuming frequently with a water-tank vacuum to collect more dust from the environment, using air conditioning and keeping windows and doors closed as much as possible.

Light

The collector and the conservator inevitably develop a love-hate relationship with light. It is the entity by which a work of art or antiquity is highlighted and admired, while simultaneously acting as the agent of physical and chemical alteration of the object.[5] A textile that is subject to light is deteriorating progressively, its colors are fading and chemical reactions (accelerated by the component of light) are set into motion. For example, the iron salts in the mordants used for brown and black dyes eat away at fabrics when exposed to light.

All forms of light are damaging to textiles, but particularly those containing ultraviolet rays: sunlight and fluorescent light. The damage they cause is cumulative and non-reversible, and fabrics should be kept out of light as much as possible. (It is an interesting fact to note that in China and Japan, owners of classical hanging scrolls keep them rolled in boxes, bringing them out into the light only for limited periods.)[6] Ultraviolet rays can break down dyes and pigments and accelerate the oxidation of fibers. In addition, incandescent light gives off heat which also contributes to the degradation of fibers. For this reason, it is important to keep display time at a minimum (ideally no more than three months) and keep light levels in the display area quite low (5 to 10 foot-candles).

For protection from ultraviolet light rays, we must first regulate the daylight, and then the fluorescent lamps. Incandescent (tungsten) light, the ordinary household bulb, does not need to be filtered.

We remove ultraviolet radiation by passing the light, before it reaches the object, through a material transparent to visible light, but opaque to ultraviolet light.[7] To control sunlight, rays can be screened in a variety of ways: films, shades and storm-window inserts provide filtering at the point of entry into the environment. Ultraviolet absorbing filters are manufactured in these forms:

Films: Their effective life is approximately five years. There are two types of films: a polyester film which can be applied by adhesive to a window surface, and a liquid metalized coating which is painted on a window surface. (The latter was developed as an energy-conservation measure and is meant to retain heat as well as act as screening.)

Shades: These have a limited life span. There is a Mylar (polyester film) plastic shade that can be pulled up and down a window exactly like a cloth shade. It is transparent and innocuous.

Storm-window inserts: These are effective for lifetime exposure. A rigid Plexiglas sheet (of UF-3 acrylic) is cut to the form of an outer storm window or interior barrier and is inserted into the existing window frame.

If, for some reason, it is not feasible to provide a filtering mechanism for the light rays, there are simple household adjustments which can help a great deal. Through a window, the light source comes from above, and the view from lower down. Some houses have shutters divided in such a way that the upper parts can be closed separately. Venetian blinds and window shades can be lowered to obscure the sky yet retain the view.[8]

Objects closest to a light source, or in the direct path of light, will be bombarded by light that exceeds the 5 to 15 foot-candle illumination level desired by museum exhibit designers. In a typical domestic room that has a combination of natural light from windows, task lighting from lamps and ambient light from simple overhead fixtures, light measurements will reveal up to 120 foot-candles at a given reading, depending on the distance of the object from the light source.

Some practical suggestions for minimizing light in a room include logical placement of the art objects out of the path of direct light and its reflected glare, keeping shades pulled down when the room is not in use and, for track lighting, substitution of low-voltage fixtures for normal incandescent line-voltage lamps. These low-voltage PAR 36 fixtures accept bulbs which will provide as much light at 50 watts as is gleaned from a 75-watt line-voltage incandescent bulb, while filtering out infrared and ultraviolet light rays.

For the control of ultraviolet emissions from fluorescent lamps, UV filter sleeves are available from various suppliers. The sleeves come in various sizes, and their filtering properties are similar to Plexiglas UF-3. You can also buy a fluorescent lamp which fits into ordinary fluorescent fixtures, requires no sleeves or filters and contains inherent UV filtering capacity.

Cleaning

Although a good cleaning may appear to be just what the quilt needs, a philosophical approach is more prudent. That is, we must accept what time has done to the piece as part of the life of the piece and even, in some cases, as an enhancer of its beauty. This principle may save the quilt from over-zealous wet cleaning, destructive bleaching or pointless dry cleaning. There are three generally accepted methods for the cleaning of a textile.

Vacuuming: The one kind of cleaning virtually all textiles can withstand is vacuuming. This must be done with caution, however.

The quilt should first be laid on a clean table and covered with Fiberglas screening, the edges of which have been covered to protect the fabric from being torn. Some fabrics are strong enough to allow you to dispense with the need for a screen. Using a low-suction, hand-held vacuum (a Hoover Porta-Power works well) and a small brush attachment, gently pass the vacuum over the top side of the quilt. Turn back one-half of the quilt, vacuum the table, then repeat this process for the other half. Turn the quilt and clean its back. This is not a difficult or uncertain procedure, but nevertheless must be done slowly and with care so that the textile is not sucked up into the vacuum or scraped or ripped by the screen. Just make certain that your small brush attachment is clean before applying it to your quilt.

A regular program of vacuuming (once every six months) for those textiles exposed to air pollution is a good maintenance measure. The dust and surface dirt that can be removed by vacuuming might otherwise cause physical abrasion and chemical damage.

Wet cleaning: A great many of the quilts that find their way into collections are not in pristine condition. They may contain areas that are ripped or frayed, have lost sewing and quilting, possess shifted batting, stains, holes or dyes that have bled. The collector's natural response is to seek to repair or eradicate many of these visually disturbing elements.

There is increasing evidence, however, that immersion in water causes a breakdown in cellulosic fibers (cotton and linen); this is reason to strike a very cautious note among conservators and collectors about the advantages of wet cleaning. There are cases where the disadvantages of a highly acidic content in the cloth are weighed against this. It may be that a textile conservator will test the pH of a fabric and make a decision to wet clean or not, based on a few important scientific notations — tests that are generally unavailable to the home collector.

There are other factors that may also affect the decision to wet clean: no previous evidence of washing, a fabric that has been glazed, a dye that appears unstable, fibers that are extensively deteriorated, the presence of weighted silks or fugitive dyes in woolen yarns and inked signatures and legends.

The best contribution of the professional conservator in such cases may be fortitude and insistence in prescribing non-treatment. I do not believe that wet cleaning is at its best in a bathroom, kitchen or outdoor tub, and because it is during this state that the quilt is at its most vulnerable, I have adopted a negative point of view about the casual wet cleaning of historic quilts in the home.

Dry cleaning: Although dry cleaning is a theoretical alternative, it is important to find a dry-cleaning machine which does not tumble its contents — an almost non-existent piece of equipment. Furthermore, the effectiveness of the dry-cleaning process is almost directly related to the amount of agitation the piece receives and, therefore, the cleaning effects of non-movement may be negligible except in special circumstances. Also, the long-term, possibly negative effects of dry-cleaning solvents on a textile have not been documented. Naturally, a decision about whether to wet or dry clean a quilt must be undertaken on a completely individual basis.

Pest Control

Mice, rats, rodents, chipmunks and squirrels, as well as other small omnivorous mammals, must be denied access to collections, particularly in winter, when they may be looking for a warm, sheltered house. All holes in the perimeter of a building should be

How to Fold and Store a Quilt

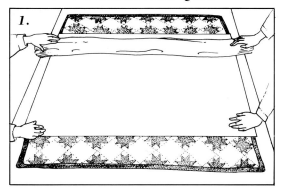

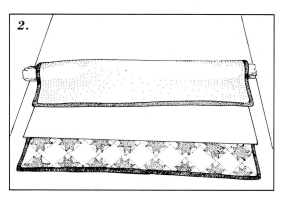

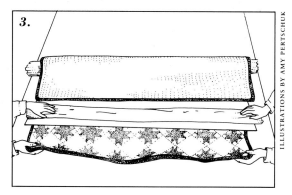

ILLUSTRATIONS BY AMY PERTSCHUK

1. Lay the quilt top-up on a clean surface. Place a sheet of acid-free tissue paper on the center of the quilt. Place a roll of crumpled

acid-free tissue paper across the top portion of the quilt so that the upper third of the quilt can be folded over the roll. 2. The upper third

folded over the roll. 3. Place another roll of paper across the quilt, so that the lower third of the quilt can be folded over this roll.

---

patched. Screens or wire grids can be strategically placed over all indoor/outdoor passages. Although these creatures do not actually feed on textiles, they search them out for perfect nest-making materials and chew through them in pursuit of foodstuffs. Commercial poisoned baits will provide security against many of these pests.[9]

The attic is a prime location for insects. Old cardboard boxes with bits and pieces of silk, wool, lint and dust kept in dark, humid environments are breeding grounds for collection-destroying insects. Fur coats, feathers, wool, silk and leather are attractive to pests that may enter the house through unscreened windows, doors or on the clothes of traffickers. Protein-eating insects will even be attracted to dead flies, so periodic vacuuming is essential.

Even elsewhere in the house, insect pests like dark, warm, undisturbed environments. Routine vigilance and careful vacuuming can remove eggs, larvae and cocoons as well as dead insects. The use of moth crystals is recommended as a pesticide when there is active

infestation. The textile can be placed in two layers of polyethelene bags in which has also been placed a packet of para-dichlorobenzene (not to be confused with naphthalene) crystals wrapped in acid-free tissue paper. For a thirty-gallon bag, approximately one-half pound of para-dichlorobenzene crystals should more than do the job. Make sure the crystals are on top of the textile as vapors proceed downward, and make sure the crystals are not in actual contact with the quilt. Seal the bag with tape, creating an air-tight chamber, and leave it for one week. A 70° temperature is best for this procedure. Sometimes it is difficult to distinguish live infestation from old damage; a prudent approach is to call an exterminator, who will be willing to identify the exact pest you have and the safest product or technique to use with material objects.

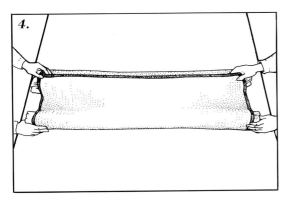

4.

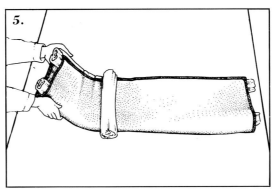

5.

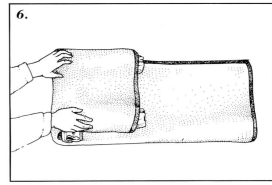

6.

4. *Fold the lower third over the roll. 5. Place a shorter roll across the folded quilt, so that*

the left side can be folded toward the center.

6. *Fold the left side toward the center.*

Storage

Ideally, flat textiles are best stored unfolded, flat and unstacked. In practice, however, this is rarely possible, since large pieces such as quilts, coverlets and counterpanes require spaces that are enormous and facilities which are absurdly expensive. Even when flat storage is modified, very few homes can accomodate specially fabricated storage units or shelving. Existing furniture has to be used or simple wooden structures built. The resulting facilities allow rolled or folded methods of storage. If an existing clothes or linen closet, armoire or chest of drawers is being converted for storage, it should be lined with acid-free barrier paper.[10] If wood is used to construct a new storage structure or container, it should be carefully sealed with several coats of polyurethane varnish before it is lined with acid-free barrier paper.

Boxed/containerized storage of individual textiles in acid-free materials is another good form of storage. Acid-free boxes are made in many sizes appropriate for historic quilts. It is actually preferable to provide folded rather than rolled storage for multi-layered textiles such as quilts. Rolling can cause buckling and strain on the various layers, and quilts with thick stuffed work can be mashed. You may also find pieces that have been too badly distorted from use or hanging to withstand rolling without forming creases, and pieces with multiple linings or uneven old repairs can present problems if rolled. When folding a quilt for storage, all folds should be well-padded with crumpled acid-free tissue paper. The folded quilt can then be stored in an acid-free box.

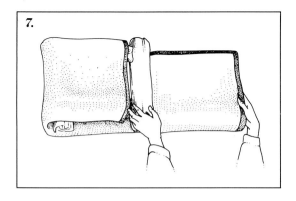

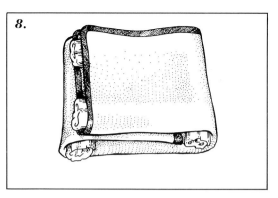

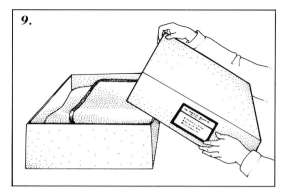

7. *Place another short roll across the folded quilt, so that the right side can be folded*

toward the center. 8. *The folded quilt, ready for storage.* 9. *The folded quilt in an acid-*

free box. The box is marked with a label, describing its contents.

In the case, however, of some large, flat, *single*-layered objects of cotton, linen or wool, rolled storage can provide very decent protection. These would include quilt tops, embroidered blankets, woven coverlets, candlewick spreads and stenciled counterpanes. During rolling, any pile or decorative elements should be on the outside of the roll. Large-diameter tubes, at least 4½", should be used whenever possible, and these should have sufficient tube-wall strength to prevent them from collapsing. If acid-free rollers are not available, numerous ways of covering the cardboard (which is itself highly acidic) are possible. These include acid-free barrier paper, acid-free tissue paper, washed muslin and polyurethane varnish. The decision of how to prepare the roller can depend on the need for a slippery or slightly rough or padded surface, concerns about excessive humidity collection on the inside of the rolled fabric and your resources. The rolled textiles should be covered with acid-free tissue or washed cotton fabric. The rollers can be suspended from racks or chains, or laid flat on a padded shelf.

Materials used in storage: If acid-free materials are unavailable, cotton sheets or washed, unbleached muslin can be used to wrap, pad and protect the textiles. In fact, some acid-free papers may not be safe for use with wool and silk because of their high buffer content. In these cases, washed cotton fabric may be preferable. Washed cotton-polyester sheets can serve as a practical substitute in all these cases.

When dust and dirt are a serious problem, plastics are useful materials, particularly as dust curtains in storage. Heavy polyethylene sheeting is generally considered safe, as well as polyester materials such as Mylar and Fiberfill. Other types of plastic have harmful vapors or degradation products. Vinyl chloride, urethane foams and Styrofoam are not safe, nor are garment bags, dry cleaners' bags or other store-bought bags.

The use of poor-quality papers can result in the slow deterioration of textiles stored in them. This deterioration is caused by the liberation of destructive by-products during the aging of the paper. Stains can also result from such deterioration. "An example of this accelerated aging can be seen in newsprint decay."[11]

Hanging a Quilt with Velcro

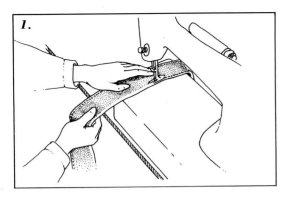

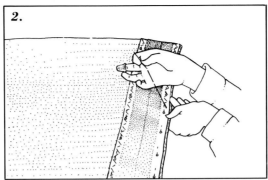

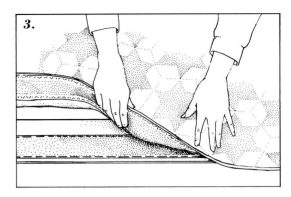

1. *Machine-sew two-inch-wide, soft-sided Velcro to three-inch-wide, washed cotton webbing which is slightly shorter than the length of the top edge of your quilt. Sew all sides of the Velcro to the webbing. 2. Hand-sew all sides* *of the webbing to the top edge of the quilt (just inside the binding) with a combination running-backstitch and herringbone stitch. These stitches go through the three layers of the quilt. [Using a staple gun, attach the hook-* *sided Velcro to a sealed wooden board, both being the same length as the webbing.] 3. Attach the Velcro strips to each other. The quilt can now be hung.*

Seepages from wood can also stain textiles. A polyester resin coating which is painted on, or sheets of polyester film which form a taped barrier, may be used to protect the textile from possible staining or other damage. Polyester serves as a better barrier than polyurethane of the same thickness because of its superior vapor permeability.[12]

Labeling: Documentation should be a part of the storage process. If you have historic information about the quilt, such as a date, the maker's name or area of origin, it should be written on a small piece of acid-free paper or washed cotton, and attached with cotton thread, loosely basted to the quilt. If the quilt is in a box, a label on the outside of the box can minimize unnecessary handling. Remove any labels attached with safety pins, straight pins, tape or staples. Historic or antique labels should be removed and placed in a fire-proof record-keeping file.

Mounting and Exhibition

To display quilts in the safest way possible, arrangements for support and suspension must be made. These may include attaching a Velcro strip, providing a lining and mounting a quilt on a framework.

Hanging a quilt with Velcro: Two-inch-wide Velcro tape can be attached by machine-sewing to a three-inch-wide, washed cotton webbing. The webbing is in turn sewn by hand to the quilt with a combination running-backstitch and herringbone stitch. These stitches go all the way through the three layers of the quilt. The hook side of the Velcro should be attached to a sealed wooden board slightly shorter in length than the top edge of the quilt. Velcro provides a quilt with continuous support for a short period of display time (three to six months). This greatly retards the likelihood of uneven stress or sagging while the textile is on display. It should be noted that the cohesion between the two sides of the Velcro can loosen. Therefore, the hanging mechanism should be periodically checked. A Velcro heading band is more effective and less intrusive on a quilt than rings, pushpins or sleeves. The piece can be stored with the Velcro strip intact.[13]

Attaching a lining: A lining of washed cotton fabric can be attached to the quilt, sewn in an even grid throughout to support the entire textile. This can be done with small stitches on the top and back, and the long threads between these stitches can be concealed between the two layers to help prevent snagging. The top and side edges of the lining are turned in and stitched, and the bottom edge is hemmed. The lining provides long-term protection for the quilt. It prevents dust and dirt accumulation on the back of the piece and potential abrasion from rubbing against a wall. More importantly, however, a lining, because of its diffused, systematic stitching pattern, creates an overall support for the quilt. It distributes the weight over the entire structure, so that no one area has to carry the weight of the whole. The value of this system is cumulative in time. Employ the Velcro hanging method described above for attaching the lined quilt to a wood support which is then hung on the wall.

Mounting a quilt on a framework: The most protective and stable mount is a sealed wooden framework (or strainer), covered with a stretched, washed cotton cloth secured to the frame back with rust-free staples. The quilt is attached to this cloth by hand-sewing in zig-zag patterns which run parallel to each other throughout the body of the quilt. This can then be covered by a Plexiglas box which does not rest on the surface of the quilt.[14] For very worn, old pieces, this gives greater overall support than the other methods and allows a quilt to be presented as a picture. It is important to note that this is the only safe method for exhibiting rare, fragile or heavy quilts. There are very precise steps to follow for this mounting process, and quilt collectors are cautioned to avoid framers who would stretch a quilt around a frame, glue the quilt to a plywood backing or sew Velcro on the quilt's four sides and stretch them to match a four-sided frame.[15]

To many readers, it may be evident that the textiles in their homes cannot be readily afforded the protective environment that we have come to expect in our museums. However, as I have outlined, almost any environment can accept some modifications. Common sense applied to preservation principles can result in a realistic method for substantial extension of life of our artifacts. Although the textile is not housed in a museum, its care and maintenance should not be considered casually, even if the object was in a pile in an antique shop until that morning. As collectors and conservators, "we have the power to change mere rags and tatters into meaningful objects."[16]

REFERENCE LIST

1. Garry Thomson, *The Museum Environment* (Boston: Butterworths, Inc., 1978), pp. 118-119.

2. "Textiles, especially those of vegetable fibers, are susceptible to attack by molds that flourish in dark, humid places with little or no ventilation. In the early

stages of mold growth, there may be a musty smell before any visible sign of deterioration appears. In the late stages of mold damage, staining occurs, which weakens the fibers and badly discolors the historic textile. This discoloration can be of greenish, yellowish or grey-brown spots that are irregular and speckled in appearance. Wet cleaning alone cannot remove this staining. Bleaching alone may be the only effective method of removing the staining, but this will further degrade the weakened cellulose and cannot be used on printed or dyed fabrics." [Margaret Fikioris, "Textile Conservation for Period Room Settings in Museums and Historic Houses," *Preservation of Paper and Textiles of Historic and Artistic Value, II*, ed. John C. Williams, Advances in Chemistry Series, No. 193 (Washington, D.C.: American Chemical Society, 1981), p. 258.]

3. Thomson, pp. 117-119.

4. *Ibid.*, p. 80.

5. Thomas B. Brill, *Light: Its Interaction with Art and Antiquities* (New York: Plenum Press, 1981), p. 1.

6. Thomson, p. 35.

7. *Ibid.*, p. 16.

8. *Ibid.*, p. 33.

9. Michael Bogle, "The Storage of Textiles," *Textile Conservation Notes: A Series of Fifteen Technical Leaflets* (North Andover, Massachusetts: Merrimack Valley Textile Museum, 1979), p. 5.

10. "Because most papers as well as cardboard and wood contain acid which can break down the fiber chains and lead to the deterioration of some fabrics (cotton, linen and other fabrics made of cellulosic fibers are most adversely affected), it is advisable that these materials not come in direct contact with the textile." [Karyn Jean Harris, *Costume Display Techniques* (Nashville: American Association for State and Local History, 1977), p. 62.]

11. Bogle, p. 7.

12. *Ibid.*

13. Step-by-step instructions for this method can be obtained in a reprint, "Instructions for Hanging a Textile with Velcro," from Textile Conservation Workshop, Main Street, South Salem, New York 10590.

14. "This air space serves to protect the framed textile from the possibility of condensation and its possible result in mold growth." [Fikioris, p. 258.]

15. Step-by-step instructions for this method can be obtained in a monograph, "Mounting Large Textiles (such as Quilts and Coverlets) on a Frame for Exhibition," from Division of Textiles, The Smithsonian Institution, The National Museum of History and Technology, Washington, D.C. 20560.

16. Nobuko Kajitani, "Care of Fabrics in the Museum," *Preservation of Paper and Textiles of Historic and Artistic Value*, ed. John C. Williams, Advances in Chemistry Series, No. 164 (Washington, D.C.: American Chemical Society, 1977), p. 162.

Supplies and Suppliers

Supplies mentioned in this article are listed below with appropriate suppliers. Other suppliers exist for some of these materials, but space permits only the following:

Mylar

Conservation Materials Ltd.
Doug and Dorothy Adams
Box 2884
340 Freeport Boulevard
Sparks, Nevada 89431
702/331-0582

and

TALAS
Division of Technical Library Service
130 Fifth Avenue
New York City, New York 10011

PAR 36 Fixtures	Litelab 76 Ninth Avenue New York City, New York 10011	Polyethylene	Conservation Materials Ltd. and Westchester Plastics 33 Carleton Avenue Mount Vernon, New York 10550
UV Filters for fluorescent lamps	For your local distributor, write or call: Rohm and Haas Company 6th and Independence Mall Philadelphia, Pennsylvania 19105 215/592-3000	Velcro	For the regional office in your area, write or call: Velcro USA Inc. Sales & Marketing P.O. Box 5218 406 Brown Avenue Manchester, New Hampshire 03108 603/669-4892
Fluorescent Lamps with inherent UV filtering capacity	Verilux, Inc. 35 Mason Street Greenwich, Connecticut 06830		
pH Paper	Conservation Materials Ltd.		
Acid-free Products	Conservation Materials Ltd. and Process Materials 30 Veterans Boulevard Rutherford, New Jersey 07070		
Acid-free Cardboard Tubing	Conservation Materials Ltd.		
Cardboard Tubing	Hudson Paper Company 30 Furler Street Totowa, New Jersey 07512 and Kern and Son, Inc. 250 W. Broadway New York City, New York 10013		

PATSY ORLOFSKY is one of America's most respected quilt historians, conservators and writers. *Quilts in America*, which she co-authored with her late husband, Myron, is regarded by many as the finest general text in the field. For the past seven years she has served as Director of the Textile Conservation Workshop in South Salem, New York. In that position, she has cared for some of this country's finest institutional and private quilt collections. This article marks her return to published writing after a ten-year hiatus.

KU'U HAE ALOHA

BY ELIZABETH AKANA

HAWAI'I PONO'I, c. 1870-1880, 74 × 72 inches. An early example of the original style of Flag quilts. Private collection.

Not much has been written about Hawaiian quiltmaking. This oversight is understandable; after all, Honolulu is twenty-five hundred miles from California, and five thousand miles from the Atlantic coast. Is it any wonder that only scant information has filtered through to the Mainland from the Islands? Even in Hawaii, a great mystery shrouds the Hawaiian quilt and its history. Families rank their ancestors' quilts among their most cherished possessions. Seldom do friends or neighbors get to see these hidden treasures, even less an outsider from afar. As a result, misinformation abounds and myth has taken the rightful place of fact. But public interest in these Island treasures is on the rise, and information is replacing hearsay.

When I began this article on the Royal Hawaiian Flag quilt, I thought for a brief moment that I had an easy task at hand. After all, I have been involved with Hawaiian quilting for thirteen years and have read all there is on the subject, or so I thought. After compiling all my information about the Flag quilt, I had a whopping two-and-a-half paragraphs. Back to the libraries, this time to read journals and diaries of early visitors, almanacs, newspapers and history books. What I discovered in the course of this research places the Royal Hawaiian Flag quilt in a different perspective, giving it new meaning.

To begin with, stitchery is documented in the Islands as early as 1809, not after the arrival of the American missionaries as previously recorded. One journal of that date uncovered in my searches notes that native tailors did their work as perfectly as Europeans.[1] In 1817, three years before the missionaries arrived, it was recorded that an *alii* (chief) stitched a coat of English cloth and that Hawaiian women were wearing robe-like calico dresses.[2] The Islands were a major link in the Pacific trade route, and Hawaiians were well-informed regarding other cultures. The women were fashion-conscious and must have been excited to learn that missionary women were on the Thaddeus, an American vessel.

It has long been known that the Thaddeus arrived on April 3, 1820, and a group of four high-ranking Hawaiian women went out

Ku'u Hae Aloha, date uncertain, 80 × 80 inches. Exemplary of one of the earliest Flag quilt styles. It is thought to have been made especially for Charles Reed Bishop and the Honorable Pauahi (Mrs. Bishop, a royal high chiefess related to the monarch). Mr. Bishop was a banker and a member of the royal government before annexation. The initials of the honored couple, as well as the two pair of crossed flags, were apparently added to an earlier design that was copied, and elaborated upon, for this quilt. Private collection.

THE MOKIHANA CLUB, Kauai, on March 1, 1933. The group was preparing for a quilt exhibition of over one hundred quilts. This old publicity photograph for that exhibition is courtesy of the Kauai Museum, Lihue.

to greet the missionary women. Their hope was that these new visitors could help them design and make a new dress in the latest fashion for Kalakua, the dowager queen, a member of their party. I can only imagine the surprise and sheer delight of the missionary women when greeted by Hawaiian women who brought with them their own cloth. They set to work immediately, but since only a few women were required to make the dress, the others, not to be slighted, were taught the art of patchwork.[3] This was the first teaching/learning exchange between the Hawaiians and the missionaries.

After establishing schools and a written language, the missionaries began teaching the Hawaiians some mainland domestic arts. Stitchery techniques were taught, including the patchwork that was first demonstrated on the Thaddeus. It is probable that the missionaries also introduced paper-cutting techniques. Paper-cutting was a highly-prized domestic art on the mainland at this time. And it is the method employed by the Hawaiians to cut the large, beautiful designs used in most of their quilts. The Hawaiians quickly brought their own expressions of the Islands — the flora and fauna — to the folded fabric. Since the quilts the Hawaiians were learning to make were not needed for warmth, their utilitarian value was limited. Consequently, they soon developed into bold creative statements. These works of art became prized possessions, most often given as gifts of love.

All Hawaiian quilts convey messages of love, capture feelings or record moments in time. With stitchery and the manipulation of fiber and color, the Hawaiians have recorded history and preserved meaningful symbols. Dorothy B. Barrere expressed it well in her article "Hawaiian Quilting: A Way of Life":

> The story of quilt making in Hawaii is a story of a way of life that was but a continuation and modernization of old ways. Innovations of materials, of techniques, of inspirational designs, were all assimilated and adapted in harmony with the age-old foundation of Hawaiian poetic thought and skill and regard for spiritual meaning.[4]

UNIQUE DESIGN, c. 1870-1880, 63 × 86 inches. This unusual example of the 1845-style Flag quilt takes artistic license with the Hawaiian flag and uses only the center crest of the coat of arms. Private collection.

This sharing and giving was seldom daunted by lack of supplies. If they lacked fabric, they would stitch together pieces of the same color, or use three or more colors instead of the traditional two seen in most Hawaiian quilts. Batting for their quilts included wool, home-grown cotton, *pulu* from the *hapu'u* tree fern and domestic animal hair. This willingness to use whatever supplies they had at hand underscores the importance of the message rather than the materials in each quilt. It seems natural then that the Royal Hawaiian flag, a beloved symbol of this island kingdom, would be captured and preserved this way.

IT has been generally accepted by historians that the Royal Hawaiian Flag quilt did not appear until 1893. This theory was stated by Stella M. Jones, a pioneer in the study of the Hawaiian quilt:

> The most beloved design, however, is *Ku'u Hae Aloha* (My Beloved Flag). Upon abdication of the Queen and the consequent lowering of their flag many of the Hawaiian people feared that they would not again be permitted to fly the emblem of their kingdom. They turned to the quilt as a means of perpetuating the flag and coat-of-arms, and the result was My Beloved Flag, a design held so sacred as never to be put to common use.[5]

However, the close parallel between the numerous pattern variations and the chronological changes in the Hawaiian flag and coat of arms leads me to believe that *Ku'u Hae Aloha* appeared as early as 1843. Stitchery skills were certainly well established by this time, and quilts must have been vehicles of Hawaiian expression by 1835. A likely date for the appearance of the Royal Hawaiian Flag quilt is 1843, since it was then that the beloved flag of the island kingdom was first removed. Just as a wave of pride washed over the Islanders with the forced abdication of their queen in 1893, so equal passions were undoubtedly stirred in 1843.

On February 25 of that year, Lord George Paulet of the British Navy claimed possession of the Sandwich Islands, as they were then known, for Great Britain. The claim was made as a result of a land dispute between the Island's king and the local British consul. The seven-striped Hawaiian flag, the standard of its people since approximately 1812, was lowered with this loss of independence. Its Union Jack canton denoted the friendship felt for that other island kingdom, Great Britain. Its seven stripes represented the seven major islands under the direct rule of King Kamehameha I. (The island of Kauai was allowed to be a tributary kingdom.[6]) This presumptive British claim of sovereignty was resolved on July 31, 1843, when Britain's Admiral Thomas restored the Hawaiian flag and forfeited Paulet's claim.

The Royal Hawaiian Flag quilt that would have appeared in 1843 was, in most probability, composed of four seven-striped flags with a crown or other royal symbol at its center. Several examples of such a design have been found in the Islands. However, all the examples I have seen were most likely made after 1870, and their flags possess eight stripes. (See photographs on pages 70 and 71.)

There are simple reasons for both these apparent discrepancies. Environmental problems are at fault, particularly the Islands' high humidity, the resultant mildew and large pest infestations. Fabric deteriorates in the Islands alarmingly, and storage usually only intensifies the rate of decay. It is reasonable, therefore, to deduce that few, if any, quilts from the 1840's have survived to the present day. Indeed, it is rare to find a Hawaiian quilt that pre-dates 1875. As a result, it is an Island tradition to copy old, deteriorating quilts before discarding them. Thus, the second discrepancy, that all Royal Hawaiian Flag quilts found to date possess eight-striped flags, is explained by the fact that the eighth stripe was added to the Hawaiian flag in 1845. Hence, copies of the earliest (1843 and 1844) Flag quilts might reflect that addition.

It was on May 25, 1845, just two years after the Paulet incident, that the Legislative Council opened by unfurling this new eight-striped Hawaiian flag.[7] The added stripe reflected Kauai's altered status. It was this same council that adopted a coat of arms brought

GREG VAUGHN

NANI AHIAHI, c. 1915, 78 × 78 inches. A copy of an 1845-style quilt with an early coat of arms. Collection of Mission Houses Museum, Honolulu.

back from Great Britain.[8] Many examples of the Royal Hawaiian Flag quilt using this coat of arms (composed of a single crown over a crest) and eight-striped flags exist. (See photograph on page 73.) Some renditions include the crest's two guards. (See photograph on page 74.)

No further changes to the Flag quilt seem to have occurred until 1883, when King Kalakaua introduced a new, more ornate coat of arms on the invitation to his coronation. The two guards were faced out, rather than in, and a formée cross was placed under the crest. An ermine cape replaced a feather one, and a second, larger crown was superimposed over all.[9] (See photograph on this page.) The Flag quilts displaying this elaborate coat of arms are the most numerous. Given our knowledge of the environmental factors prevalent in the Islands, this is not surprising.

Annexation to the United States in 1898 was a final, new theme to incorporate into the Royal Hawaiian Flag quilt. Varying interpretations of this theme exist. (See photograph on page 76.) However, there are few pattern duplications. It would seem, therefore, that this was not a popular design, and understandably so. After all, Hawaiians loyal to their last queen and her family might not want to incorporate the American flag into their beloved quilts.

VERY few Royal Hawaiian Flag quilts have been found on the Mainland. The Hawaiians, who treasure these quilts above all others, have given away very few to Mainlanders returning home. Indeed, relatively few are displayed in Hawaiian museums. Thus, it has been concluded that the Flag quilts are rare in number. However, during my investigations, I found that most native families that own Hawaiian quilts have at least one Flag quilt, and often more. These quilts are zealously guarded family treasures, passed from generation to generation, and thus their very existence has been kept a secret. In fact, the *mana* (spirit) of a quiltmaker is often believed to rest in a finished quilt. Many quiltmakers presumably

KU'U HAE ALOHA, 1899, 82 × 88 inches. The people of Palāma Mission, Honolulu, made this quilt as a remembrance gift for Anne Pope before she left her position as its first kindergarten director because of failing health. In the same year that she returned to the Mainland, the mission was nearly decimated by the bubonic plague. Many of the women who worked on the quilt lost their lives. The settlement was rebuilt and flourishes today. Collection of Sally Auner, Dallas, Texas.

ANNEXATION DESIGN, c. 1900-1920, 82 × 79 inches. Note that the American flag has twelve stars and eleven stripes and that the Hawaiian flag has thirteen stripes. The message of the quilt, not its numerical accuracy, was obviously the quiltmaker's goal. Collection of the author.

left instructions for their creations to be burned at their deaths. This practice of protecting one's *mana* continues, in some cases, today.

Much has been learned about these unique quilts, and there is a great deal left to discover. We can be certain, however, that the first of these quilts dates from before 1893. Numerous examples exist which can be unmistakably placed between 1870 and 1890. Some of these Flag quilts carry complete documentation proving their age

THE ROYAL HAWAIIAN family and friends, August 2, 1898. Front row from left to right: Joe Heleluhe, Prince David Kawanakakoa, Princess Kaiulani, Queen Liliuokalani (seated), Prince Kuhio, Mrs. James O. Carter and Mrs. Sarah Babbit. One senses the anguish of this group that welcomed the Queen back from her trip to Washington, D.C. She had traveled the long distance to see if some sympathy could be raised for the Island kingdom and her throne. However, her trip was fruitless; annexation was celebrated ten days later. Photograph courtesy of the Bishop Museum, Honolulu.

and authenticity. Thus, the widely-held belief that the up-heavals of 1891 and the abdication of Queen Liliuokalani in 1893 inspired these wonderful quilts is false. It may be that we will never ascertain the exact date of their origin, but Hawaiian changes in style between 1843 and the turn of the century are undeniably catalogued in the decorated tops of these quilts. The progression of change that they chronicle cannot be disregarded.

The pride and dignity of a past culture is captured forever in these dramatic quilts. We see it, and feel it, as we read the inscriptions found on many of them: *Ku'u Hae Hawai'i* (My Hawaii Flag), *Hawai'i Pono'i* (Hawaii's Own), *Nani Ahiahi* (Beautiful Evening) and *Ku'u Hae Aloha* (My Beloved Flag). The Royal Hawaiian Flag quilt is a fitting legacy of America's only royal family.

THE ROYAL HAWAIIAN flag is lowered on August 12, 1898, during annexation ceremonies. Photograph courtesy of the Bishop Museum, Honolulu.

REFERENCE LIST

1. Archibald Campbell, *A Voyage Round The World, from 1806 to 1812* (Honolulu: University of Hawaii Press, 1967), p. 144.

2. V.M. Golovnin, *Around The World On The Kamchatka 1817-1819* (Honolulu: The University Press of Hawaii, 1979), p. 178.

3. Kym Snyder Rice, "The Hawaiian Quilt," *Art & Antiques*, May/June 1981, p. 102.

4. Dorothy B. Barrere, "Hawaiian Quilting: A Way of Life," *The Conch Shell*, III, 2 (1964), 21.

5. Stella M. Jones, *Hawaiian Quilts*, revised edition (Honolulu: Honolulu Academy of Arts, Daughters of Hawaii and Mission Houses Museum, 1973), p. 16.

6. Thomas G. Thrum, *Hawaiian Almanac* (Honolulu: Thomas G. Thrum, 1880), p. 25.

7. *Ibid.*, pp. 25-26.

8. Meiric K. Dutton, *Hawaii's Great Seal And Coat Of Arms* (Honolulu: Loomis House Press and Hale Pai O Lumiki, 1960), p. 4.

9. *Ibid.*, p. 13.

ELIZABETH AKANA is a Hawaiian quiltmaker and quilt historian who lives in Kaneohe on the island of Oahu. She is known throughout the Islands for her interest in preserving Hawaii's rich quilt heritage. She has served as curator for several quilt exhibitions in Hawaii and is the author of *Hawaiian Quilting: A Fine Art*.

SHARON RISEDORPH

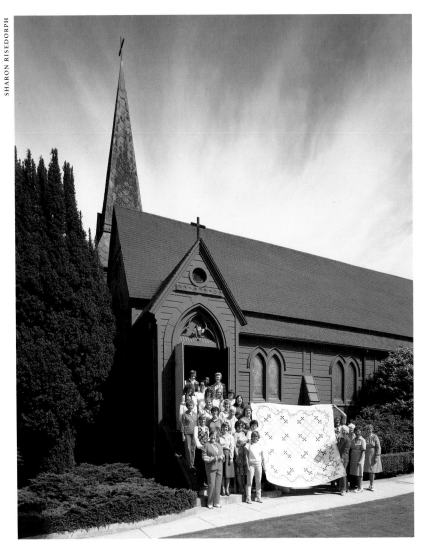

Monterey Peninsula Quilters Guild, California.

I n last year's inaugural edition, we asked our readers to write to us with their suggestions and criticisms. Many responded, and the quality of correspondence has been both heartwarming and intellectually stimulating. We thank all of you who took the time to share your ideas and comments with us. We have carefully kept a log of all praise and criticism. As a few examples of our reaction to reader suggestions, we have increased the size of this year's edition, added pages to *Showcase* and incorporated a heavier, laminated cover to protect this volume better.

Please continue the dialogue by sending us your ideas, requests and criticisms, as we look forward to incorporating many of them into future editions. We would appreciate receiving a self-addressed, stamped envelope from those expecting an editorial reply.

We cannot accept responsibility for unsolicited articles, photographs or color negatives, and cannot return them unless they are accompanied by a self-addressed, stamped envelope. We request the opportunity to hold some photographs or negatives for future editions. If you are sending photographs or negatives and do not wish us to hold them beyond a certain date, please so inform us.

We look forward to hearing from you.

Where to buy *The Quilt Digest*

HUNDREDS of quilt, antique, book and museum shops across the country carry *The Quilt Digest 1* (1983) and *The Quilt Digest 2* (1984). Check with shops in your area. Chances are that at least one of them is carrying *The Quilt Digest*. If not, you may order copies of both volumes directly from us.

To order, send us your name, address, city, state and zip code. Tell us how many copies of *The Quilt Digest 1* (1983) you want at $9.95 per copy, and how many copies of *The Quilt Digest 2* (1984) at $12.95 per copy. California residents must add 6% sales tax. Finally, add $1.50 for every copy ordered, to cover postage and handling charges. (Your books will be shipped in sturdy, beautifully-designed individual mailing cartons.) Enclose your check made payable to *Kiracofe and Kile*, and mail it, along with the above information, to 955 Fourteenth Street, San Francisco 94114.

Allow 4-6 weeks for delivery.

We are happy to send gift copies directly to recipients.

Wholesale information is available upon request.

News about *The Quilt Digest 3*

AVAILABLE in April 1985.

Work has already begun on this exciting edition. We are continuing *The Collector* and *Showcase* series. To accompany them, we have commissioned articles by a highly-talented group of quilt experts. The finely-reproduced color photographs you have come to expect from *The Quilt Digest* will also be abundant.

In February 1985, we will mail a detailed description of *The Quilt Digest 3*, in addition to complete price information, to everyone on our mailing list. If you are not already on our mailing list and wish to be, please write to us. We will be happy to add your name so that you will receive advance information about any books we publish.